THIS BOOK BELONGS TO

_____

MYSTERY MOSAICS. PASSION.
COLOR BY NUMBER BOOK FOR ADULTS.

This is a unique color by number mosaic book, where final pictures appear only after you color all square sections. Each section is 3*3 mm.

25 pictures open mostly all sides of the Passion essence. For example, for somebody music is a passion, for others — sport, old cars, travel or jewelry, etc. You will remember or recover your passion while coloring.

This process looks like Sudoku from the first side, but it is not. It's a new format of color by number mosaic book — stress relief and mind ware.

The unique palette of 22 colors (18 classics and 4 additional color shades) is easy to find in any pen, pencil or felt-tip set. Each color suits a particular number on the picture. The palette is located at the backside of the cover. In any case, you can use 18 colors, changing 4 additional shades into the similar in the palette.

This activity art book is a nice choice to spend your time during the weekend or vacations.

CONTENT

Balcony	5	**Pilotage**	31
Ballerina	7	**Podium**	33
Bulldog	9	**Poker**	35
Cabriolet	11	**Saxophonist**	37
Custom Bike	13	**Shoes**	39
Flowers	15	**Skier**	41
Formula-1	17	**Surfer**	43
Golf	19	**Tango**	45
Guitarist	21	**Travel**	47
Horse	23	**Wedding**	49
Jewelry	25	**Yacht**	51
Kiss	27	**Yoga**	53
Pianist	29		

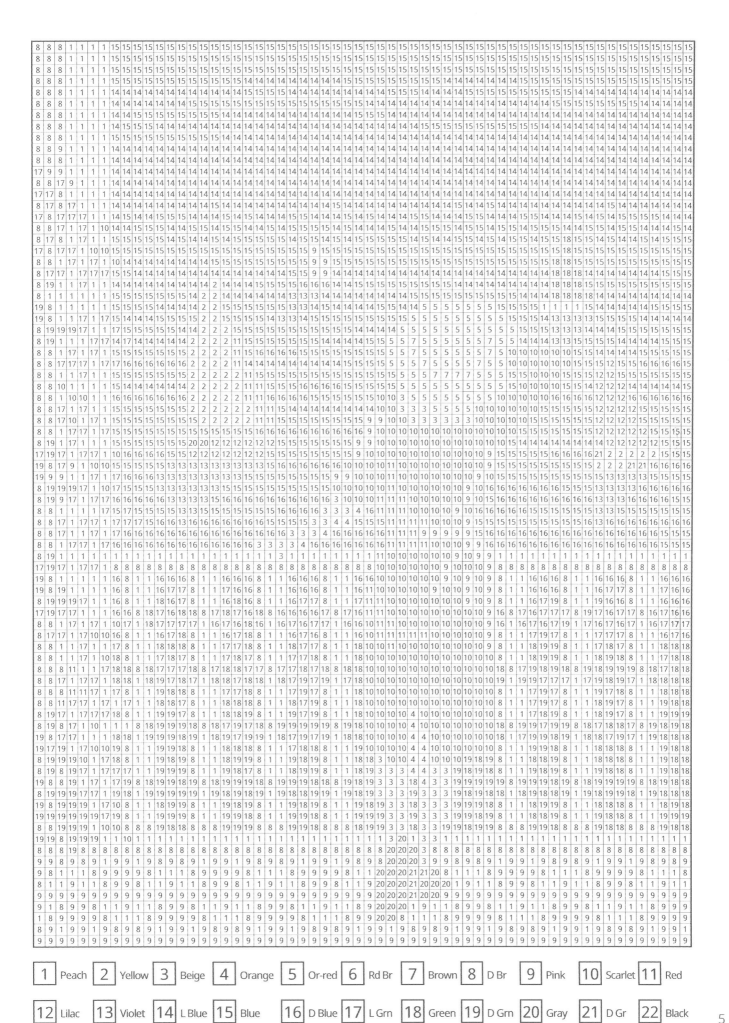

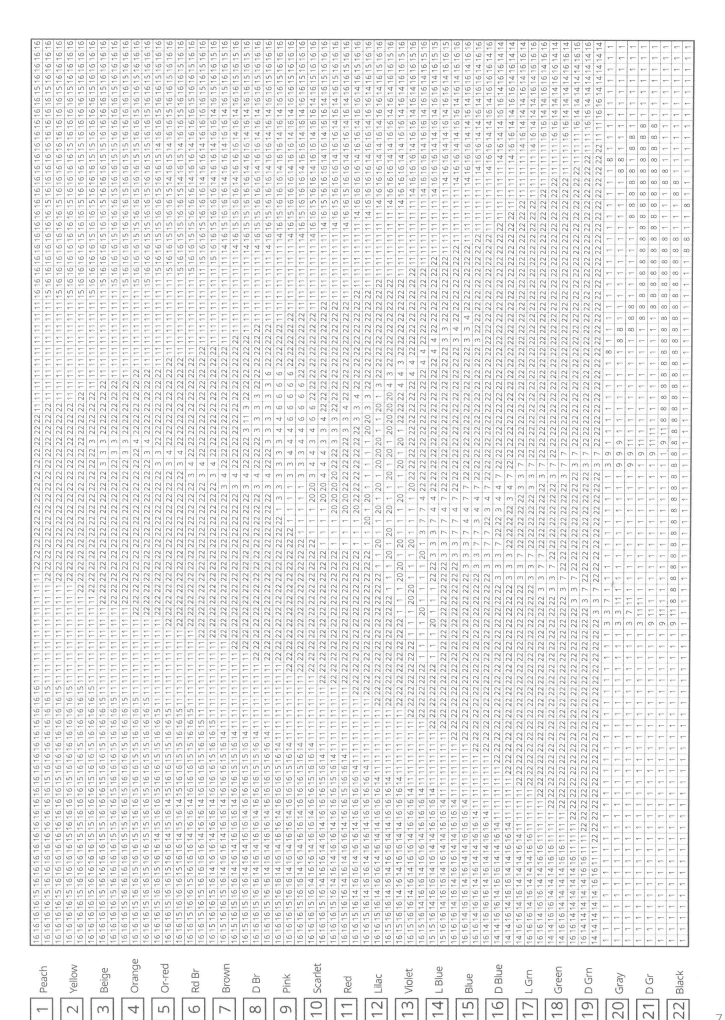

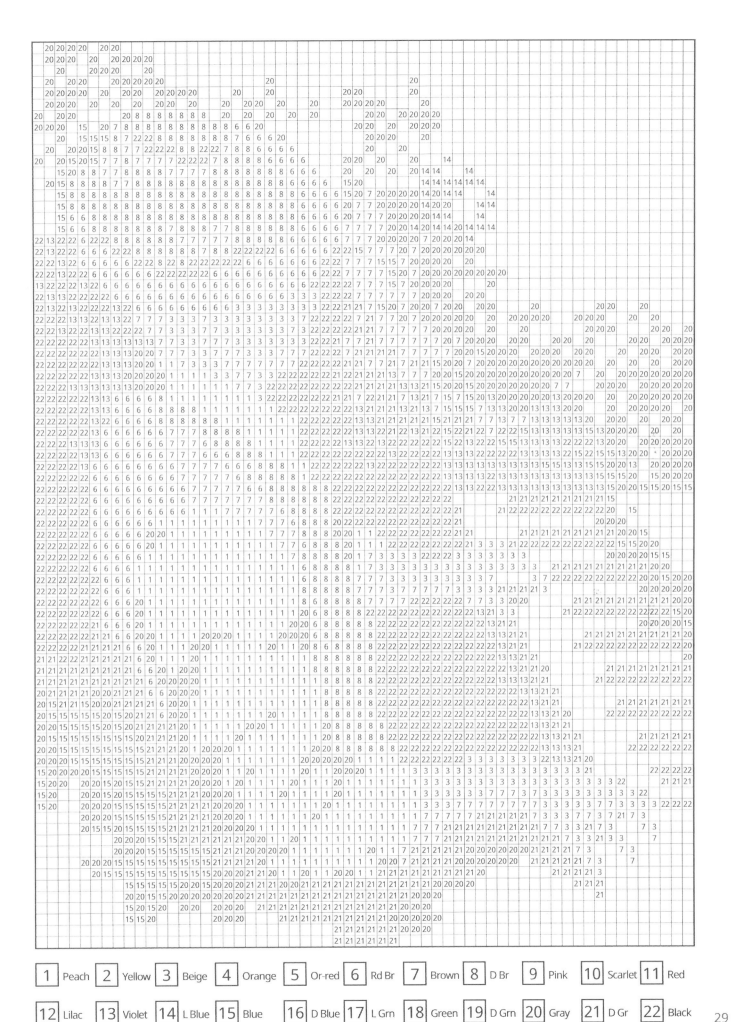

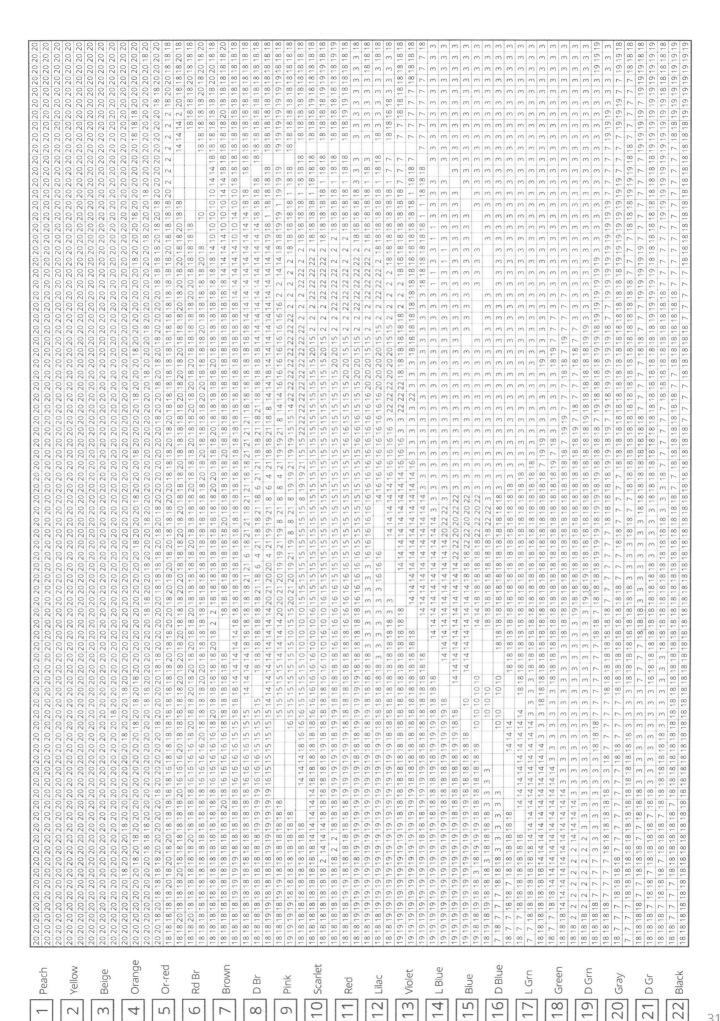

1	Peach
2	Yellow
3	Beige
4	Orange
5	Or-red
6	Rd Br
7	Brown
8	D Br
9	Pink
10	Scarlet
11	Red
12	Lilac
13	Violet
14	L Blue
15	Blue
16	D Blue
17	L Grn
18	Green
19	D Grn
20	Gray
21	D Gr
22	Black

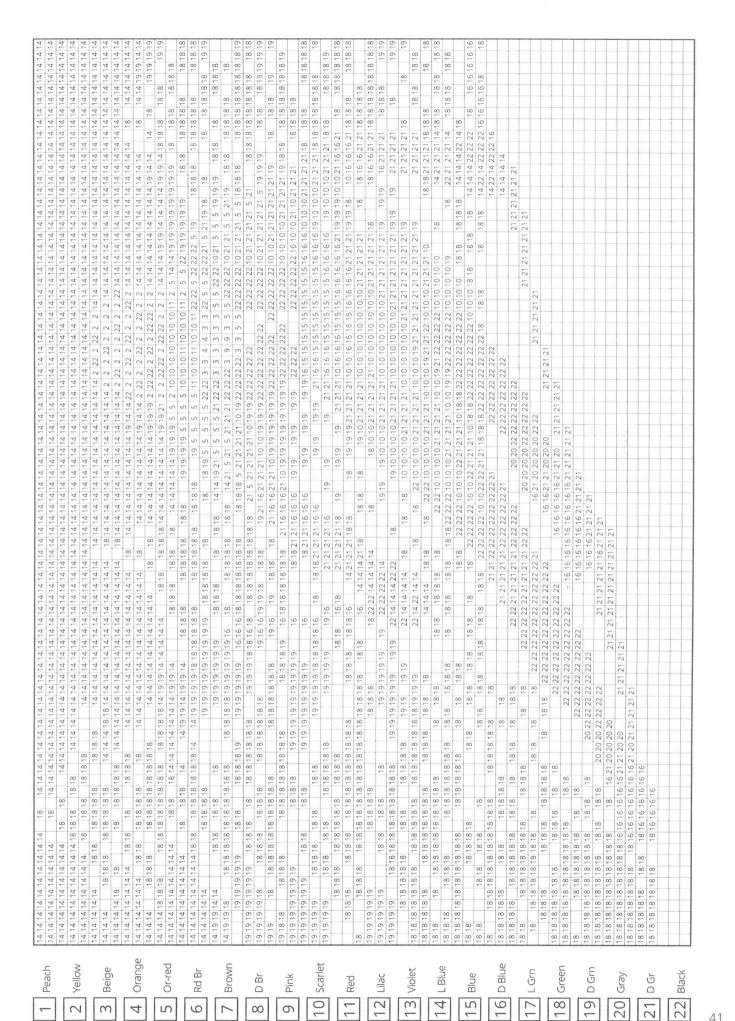

1	Peach
2	Yellow
3	Beige
4	Orange
5	Or-red
6	Rd Br
7	Brown
8	D Br
9	Pink
10	Scarlet
11	Red
12	Lilac
13	Violet
14	L Blue
15	Blue
16	D Blue
17	L Grn
18	Green
19	D Grn
20	Gray
21	D Gr
22	Black

54

WE ARE BELBA FAMILY.

All books are made with love for People and Nature.

We thank you for your choice.

And we will appreciate your feedback with a review of the book on Amazon, Facebook or Instagram.

Your opinion could help us to make our books better.

Follow us:

📘 https://www.facebook.com/belbafamily/
📷 Belba Family

Made in the USA
Las Vegas, NV
27 December 2020